ROBINS!

How They Grow Up

BY EILEEN CHRISTELOW

CLARION BOOKS : HOUGHTON MIFFLIN HARCOURT : BOSTON NEW YORK

WHO ARE WE?

We're robins!

Our black and white speckles mean we're young—a few months old. Robin teenagers!

Why are we living in your yard?

Well, here's the story.

FIRST, LET'S TELL ABOUT DAD'S LONG TRIP.

YOU MEAN BEFORE WE WERE BORN?

At the end of winter, the days stay light longer and the robins grow restless. They know it's time to start new families.

But first, they must head north, where the ground is thawing after a long winter. Soon there will be plenty of food for new babies: fat earthworms, newly hatched insects, and, in a few months, a fresh crop of fruit.

All across the country, the males set out first—millions of them, including Dad.

They stop to eat and sleep along the way. It's a dangerous and exhausting trip!

A couple of weeks and a few hundred miles later, Dad arrives in a familiar area not far from where he raised a family last year.

Now he needs to find a place to call his own.

HE LOOKED FOR SAFE PLACES TO BUILD NESTS AND TO HIDE FROM PREDATORS...

...AND FOR WATER AND GOOD WORMY SOIL!

Dad chooses a spot with plenty of trees and a lawn full of juicy worms.

"This is my place, my place, my place," he sings.

A few other males try to move in too, but Dad chases them next door.

A few weeks later, female robins show up—including Mom! She hears Dad singing and meets him over a breakfast of delicious worms. He looks strong and healthy— the perfect father for baby robins—so she sticks around. (Dad doesn't chase *her* away!)

After resting from her long trip, Mom searches for a safe place to build a nest—
somewhere protected from predators and rain. She chooses a hoe in an open shed.

She makes hundreds of trips with beakfuls of straw, twigs, dry leaves—even a piece of red string. She squishes in lots of mud with her feet and wings to hold everything together. After a few days, she has a bowl-shaped nest. When the mud is dry, she lines it with soft grasses.

A NEST IS A CRADLE...

...FOR BABY BIRDS.

Mom lays one fertile blue egg each day.
Four days later, she's ready for her next job.

Mom sits on her eggs, keeping them warm so baby birds will grow inside. She turns the eggs often so the temperature stays even—otherwise the babies might stick to the shell!

When Mom leaves the nest to find food, she can't stay away for long.

One day, when Mom is away, a squirrel invades our nest!
Luckily, Mom discovers him before he devours all the eggs.

Dad pursues him into the woods, pecking at his behind.

Now only three eggs remain.

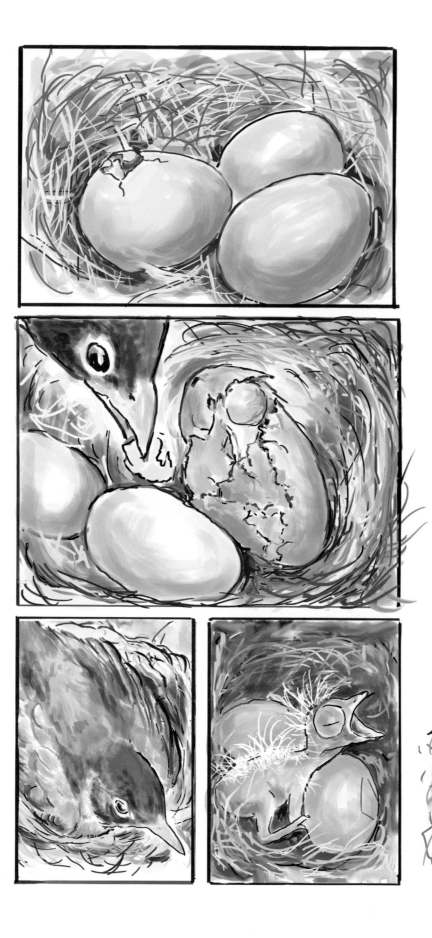

Mom sits on those eggs for thirteen days.
Then the first one she laid begins to crack.
A tiny egg tooth on a tiny beak appears.
Tap, tap, tap . . .
It's a baby! Pushing its way out!
Mom carries away bits of shell.
Then the baby needs to rest under her warmth before struggling again.

Hours later, there's an exhausted, naked baby robin, barely able to lift its head for food.

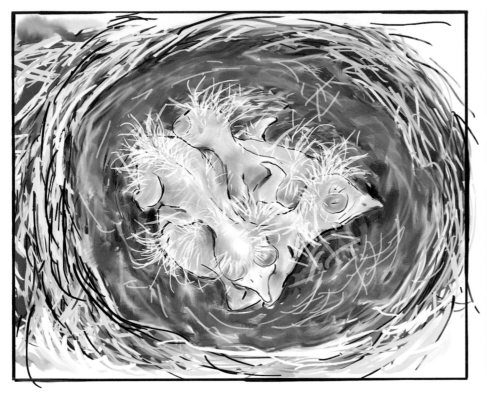

By the next day, there are three of us—a tangle of helpless babies covered with white downy fluff. Our eyes are still closed, but when we feel the nest rock slightly, we open our orange beaks wide. Is it Mom? Dad?

"Feed meee!"

We're hungry *all* the time!

WE ATE BABY FOOD!

REGURGITATED WORMS! YUM!

SIX DAYS OLD

Our eyes are open. Our feathers are just beginning to emerge. We can eat grown-up food—pieces of worms, caterpillars, and moths!

"Feed me!"

"Feed MEEE!"

Soon after we eat, we poop little white sacs, which Mom and Dad eat or carry away. They make trip after trip, back and forth, always keeping an eye on our nest.

The first week, when we don't have many feathers, Mom sits on us at night and at times during the day, keeping us warm and dry. It's cozy under there!

EIGHT DAYS OLD

More feathers!

Each one grows out in a sheath that looks like a tiny straw. As we move around, preen and scratch, the sheaths crumble into pieces . . . and our feathers unfold!

FEATHERS KEEP US WARM AND DRY . . .

. . . AND HELP US FLY!

Over two weeks, we eat about 350 insects and fourteen feet of worms—*each!* All that food makes us grow quickly. We're almost as big as Mom and Dad!

FOURTEEN DAYS OLD

For a couple of days, we've been flapping our wings and standing on the edge of the nest. Today one of us takes off!

A few hours later, another follows. Now one is left all alone.

He hears his brother calling,
so he perches on the edge of
the nest.
    It's a long way down!
    He flaps his wings . . .
pushes off . . .
    And . . . he's flying!
        Flapping . . .
            falling.
                Flying . . .
                    falling,
                        down,
                            down,
                                down.

Thwump! Hop, hop-hop . . .

Where *is* everyone?

Mom flies down. "*Chup! Chup! Chup!* Follow me!"

Then suddenly . . .

"Chip! Chip! Chip! Chip!" calls Dad. "Danger! Danger! Danger!"

Where? Our brother hops, flaps . . .

. . . and flap-flutter-flaps as fast as he can, taking refuge among some tall plants.
He stays very still, his heart pounding.
Finally, Mom shows up with a succulent moth.

FIFTEEN DAYS OLD

We're back together. Mom and Dad keep us hidden under tall plants. We're partially camouflaged by our speckled feathers. We are *helpless!* We don't know how to find food. We can barely fly. We don't know *anything!*

MOM AND DAD HAD TO TEACH US!

MOSTLY DAD. MOM WAS BUILDING A NEW NEST FOR MORE BABIES.

How do we learn to fly? We hop, run, flap, flap, flap, strengthening our wings and legs.
After a few days, we can fly short distances. Our tail feathers are still growing in.

When we can fly well enough, Dad leads us to a special tree nearby, where we spend the night with other robin dads and their kids. It's a roost—a flock of birds looking out for one another.

SLEEPING IN THE ROOST IS SAFER.

AND WE MET OTHER ROBINS!

THREE WEEKS OLD

We're stronger, bigger, and we have full tail feathers! But we still depend on Dad for food. In the early morning when he goes hunting for worms, we follow, waiting to be fed.

Dad starts dropping the worms, and we have to find them.

We poke, peck, scratch . . .

Then we learn a trick.

If we *tilt* our heads, we can see and hear better! With a little practice, we're finding moths, spiders, caterpillars . . . and *worms!*

OUR EYES ARE ON THE SIDES OF OUR HEADS.

YEAH, I'M LOOKING RIGHT AT YOU!

Six weeks old

Now we can find our own food, but it's hard work!

Sometimes we still want Dad to feed us. This time, it's our brother begging, *"Cheep-cheep!"*

Dad ignores him . . . he's listening.

"Seeee! Seeee! Seeee!" It's another robin alerting us to an intruder.

Dad darts away.

"Chip! Chip-chip-chip-chip!" he warns.

Two of us escape into a tree. But our brother continues, *"Cheep-cheep-cheep-cheeep!*

"Cheep, cheee—"

Whoosh! We hear beating wings. A hawk! A shriek.

Then it's quiet. Our brother is gone. Mom and Dad chase the hawk, scolding and screaming, but he flies away, our brother dangling from his talons—a meal for hungry hawk babies.

31

We stay very still. Eventually the shrieking stops. The woods return to normal.
We hear Dad call, *"Chip-chip, chip-chip!"*

We answer, *"Cheep, cheep, cheep!"*
It doesn't take long for him to find us.

WE WERE LEARNING ROBIN-TALK . . .

. . . SO WE COULD COMMUNICATE WITH OTHER ROBINS.

Dad leads us to a nearby stream. We flap and splash, ruffling our feathers so the water gets down to our skin. We feel much better.

We dry off in the sun, preening—oiling, smoothing, and realigning our feathers and nibbling away any remaining dirt or itchy fleas.

Eight weeks old

We're almost grown up! We spend our days flying around with friends from the roost, always watching the older robins: listening and learning.

WE WERE LEARNING HOW TO BE ROBINS.

WE'RE STILL LEARNING!

If we hear a mob of scolding robins, we fly over to watch . . . from a safe distance.

Usually, they're hassling the neighborhood owl.

THEY DIDN'T WANT HIM NEAR THEIR NESTS . . .

. . . BECAUSE HE MIGHT EAT THEIR BABIES!

THREE MONTHS OLD

Now there are more robins around! New fledglings and the moms have joined us.

There won't be any more babies or nest-building until next year. The robins aren't squabbling over territory or protecting new broods. They're friends again, moving around together.

Then we make another discovery!

WE ALWAYS WATCHED TO SEE WHERE THE OLDER ROBINS FOUND FOOD.

WE SAW THEM HANGING OUT IN THAT TREE.

We fly over and find them grabbing crabapples! We watch carefully, then try to grab some too. Picking fruit is almost as tricky as catching worms! At first, it's easier to eat what drops on the ground.

NOW WE'RE EATING CRABAPPLES AND BERRIES.

AS IT GETS COLDER, WORMS AND INSECTS WILL DISAPPEAR.

FIVE MONTHS OLD

The robins are getting ready for winter. We're stuffing ourselves with food, growing fatter and stronger. And we're molting: replacing old, worn-out feathers with new ones.

Everyone is restless. Is something about to change?

With fresh new feathers to keep us warm, we could stay here all winter! But in cold northern winters, worms burrow deep underground and insects disappear. There is less fruit left on the trees.

So most of our flock start to wander south, where our favorite foods will be easier to find.

Of course, we follow.

AND THAT'S OUR LIFE... SO FAR!

WE'LL BE BACK NEXT YEAR!

Author's Note

Early in May several years ago, a robin built a nest on a hoe in our garden shed. My husband, needing the hoe, moved the nest. The robin immediately built another nest on the same hoe before he could even use it.

"You can borrow a hoe," I suggested. "Building a nest is hard work, and for some reason, she's determined to start her family on *your* hoe."

For the next four weeks, if we entered our shed to find a rake or a shovel, the mother robin would make a harried exit to a nearby tree. Then she and her mate would chastise us until we exited.

In spite of the scolding, we'd quickly peek at the nest. It was above eye level, so we could only guess what was going on inside of it. And then . . . at the end of the fourth week, we noticed three fully feathered little birds standing at the edge, peering down at us.

Two days later, they were gone!

What happened in that nest during those four weeks? Where did those little birds go? I started reading about robins, and this project began.

As a result, over the last few years, I've been taking more notice of the life going on in our surrounding woods. I hope this book will encourage others to do the same.

GLOSSARY:
Do you know these words?

BROOD—A family of young birds produced at one hatching.

BROOD PATCH—The featherless patch of skin on the mother bird's belly, which she uses to warm her eggs. After nesting season, the feathers grow back.

CAMOUFLAGE—An animal's coloring that helps it to blend in with its surroundings, making it more difficult to see.

EGG TOOTH—A hard bump on a baby bird's beak that it uses to crack out of its shell. The egg tooth drops off shortly after hatching.

FLEDGE—When a young bird leaves the nest.

FLEDGLING—A young bird that has just left the nest.

FLOCK—A group of birds that feed, roost, and move around together.

GIZZARD—The part of a bird's stomach where muscles grind their food. (Sometimes birds swallow grit and pebbles that help with the grinding.)

INCUBATE—Keep the eggs warm so they will hatch.

MIGRATE—When birds move from one area to another, depending on the season. Most robins migrate north in the early spring and south in the late fall.

MOLT—When birds shed old feathers to make way for fresh new feathers.

PREDATOR—An animal that hunts others for food. Owls, hawks, cats, and snakes are some of the predators of robins. Robins are predators of worms and insects.

PREEN—What birds do to clean and straighten their feathers.

ROOST—Where birds settle together to sleep at night—usually in a dense group of trees or shrubs.

More About Robins!

• • •

How long do robins live?

There are so many dangers awaiting young robins that only one in four manages to survive six months. If they make it through their first year, they have a chance of living six years. The oldest wild robin known lived to be almost fourteen years old.

How big is a robin's egg? How big is a nest?

An egg is about the size of a green grape. The inside of the nest is about the size of a baseball.

How much does a newly hatched robin weigh?

Just out of the egg, she weighs about 5.5 grams—the weight of a quarter. When she leaves the nest two weeks later, she weighs ten times more—the weight of ten quarters!

Adult robins weigh 70 to 80 grams.

How many families do robins have in one season?

Robins mate once a year and usually produce two broods, sometimes three. The moms build a new nest in a different spot for each brood.

Do robins sing all year round?

The males are the singers and basically sing only during their breeding season in the early morning and evening. "*Cheerily-cheerily, cheerily-cheerup, cheerup!*" They sing to defend nesting territory and to attract a mate. Female robins communicate with short calls, which males also use: "*Chup-chup-chup-chup!*"

What do robins eat?

About 40% of their diet is earthworms and insects. The other 60% is fruit. Robins have slender beaks, which are adapted for eating soft foods. They don't eat seeds, so you won't see them at your bird feeder.

How fast can robins fly?

They can fly 20 to 30 miles per hour. They flap their wings three or four times per second.

Why do robins migrate north in the spring breeding season?

Food and more space! They have been wandering around south in large sociable flocks, eating fruit and insects.

But now they need their own nesting territories, with easy access to fresh sources of worms and insects—protein for growing babies.

WHEN ROBINS MIGRATE NORTH, DO THEY RETURN TO THEIR BIRTHPLACE?

Some do; some don't. Studies of banded robins suggest that perhaps as many as 70% return to within 10 to 20 miles of where they were born.

HOW LONG DOES IT TAKE A ROBIN TO MIGRATE SOUTH TO NORTH?

Robins follow the spring thaw, so they can be held up by a sudden drop in temperature. And they need to rest and eat! On good days, they might travel 200 miles. Depending on the weather and where they are headed, the trip can take a few days or a few weeks.

HOW DO MIGRATING ROBINS FIND THEIR WAY?

People are still trying to figure that out. Birds seem to have an inner compass. They know which way is north. Daytime migrants, like robins, can use the location of the sun to orient themselves. They can use visual landmarks, like rivers. It's possible they can orient to the earth's magnetic field.

DO ALL ROBINS MIGRATE SOUTH FOR THE WINTER?

Most fly south. However, robins are often seen in the winter in the northern United States. They can survive in cold weather as long as food—such as crabapples or sumac—is available. If a male robin sticks around for the winter, he'll have first choice of nesting territory in the spring.

HOW DO ROBINS STAY WARM IN THE WINTER?

They fluff out their down feathers, which is why they look fatter in the winter. They can maintain body heat by shivering. But they need food to create enough energy to shiver.

HOW DO ROBINS COOL OFF IN THE SUMMER?

Birds pant to eliminate body heat. (We humans sweat.)

WHEN ARE YOUNG ROBINS CONSIDERED ADULT?

A year after they hatch.

FEATHERS

Robins have about 2,900 feathers. There are *contour feathers,* which include wing, tail, and body feathers, and *down feathers,* which are underneath and keep birds warm, like a down jacket. Adult robins molt all of their feathers during the summer months. Youngsters molt their juvenile feathers but not their flight feathers.

SENSES

Robins' strongest senses are eyesight and hearing. Taste and smell are not as developed.

Sources

• • •

BOOKS

Birkhead, Tim. *Bird Sense: What It's Like to Be a Bird.* Bloomsbury, 2012.

Eiserer, Len. *The American Robin: A Backyard Institution.* Taylor Trade Publications, 1976.

Sibley, David Allen, illustrator. *The Sibley Guide to Bird Life and Behavior.* Edited by Chris Elphick, John B. Dunning, and David Allen Sibley. Alfred A. Knopf, 2001.

Wauer, Roland H. *The American Robin.* University of Texas Press, 1999.

Young, Jon. *What the Robin Knows: How Birds Reveal the Secrets of the Natural World.* Houghton Mifflin Harcourt, 2012.

WEBSITES

learner.org/jnorth/robin

toughlittlebirds.com/2013/07/10/the-fledgling-problem

Many thanks to Laura Erickson for her helpful comments.

• • •

And thanks to the robins who have nested on our window ledges and cornices; in our garage and garden shed; and—for the last three years—in the exact same spot in our wisteria.

• • •

For Ahren, who has watched the robins with me.

• • •

CLARION BOOKS

3 Park Avenue, New York, New York 10016

WWW.HMHCO.COM

The illustrations in this book were done digitally using various Photoshop brushes, an iMac, and a large Wacom Pro tablet.
The text was set in Minion Pro and Fold-and-Staple.

Library of Congress Cataloging-in-Publication Data
Names: Christelow, Eileen. | Title: Robins! : how they grow up / Eileen Christelow.
Description: Boston : Clarion Books, Houghton Mifflin Harcourt, [2016] |Audience: Age 6–9.
Identifiers: LCCN 2015051339 | ISBN 9780544442894 (hardback) | Subjects: LCSH: Robins—Juvenile literature.
Robins—Life cycles—Juvenile literature. | BISAC: JUVENILE NONFICTION / Animals / Birds. | JUVENILE NONFICTION
Science & Nature / General (see also headings under Animals or Technology). | Classification: LCC QL696.P288 C486 2016
DDC 598.8/4—dc23 | LC record available at http://lccn.loc.gov/2015051339

Manufactured in China | SCP 10 9 8 7 6 5 4 3 2 1 | 4500621656